T0193220

EXPERIENCING
GOD'S GLORY

THE PLACE, THE SITUATION, AND THE TIME

OLAYINKA ALAMU

WESTBOW
PRESS®
A DIVISION OF THOMAS NELSON
& ZONDERVAN

WestBow Press books may be ordered through booksellers or by contacting:

WestBow Press
A Division of Thomas Nelson & Zondervan
1663 Liberty Drive
Bloomington, IN 47403
www.westbowpress.com
844-714-3454

Scripture taken from the New King James Version®. Copyright © 1982 by Thomas Nelson. Used by permission. All rights reserved.

ISBN: 978-1-6642-9760-9 (sc)
ISBN: 978-1-6642-9761-6 (hc)
ISBN: 978-1-6642-9762-3 (e)

Library of Congress Control Number: 2023907023

Print information available on the last page.

WestBow Press rev. date: 07/05/2023

To my dearest wife, Adedayo, of twenty-four years and many more years to come to the glory of God. I am truly thankful for having you in my life, always believing in me, and being a great source of unconditional love and inspiration. I love you.

To our destiny boys Toluwanimi, Ibukunoluwa, and Oluwajoba. You are the manifestation of God's glory in our lives. Ever since you were born, your lives have been for signs and wonders, and you have always given your mum and me reasons to give glory to God continually. I hope this book will remind you that God created you in His glory (Isaiah 43:7) and you exist in God's glory (Ephesians 2:10) to shine for God (Matthew 5:16).

Last but not least, I am dedicating this book to my parents, Olukunle and Olabisi Alamu, and my parents-in-law, Adekunle and Ebunoluwa Adediji, for their prayers.

CONTENTS

ACKNOWLEDGMENTS

I want to thank the King of glory, the Almighty God, through Jesus and by the power of the Holy Spirit, for enabling me to start and finish this book. Second, I want to thank my wife, my destiny helper, Adedayo. From reading early drafts to giving me advice on the cover, she was as important to this book getting done as I was. Thank you so much, dear.

I want to appreciate Rev. (Dr.) Olusegun Obed, founder of Dayspring Church. You have laid the foundation of my ministry in the United States. I will never forget you for your discipline, integrity, and passion for education and research. These combinations have helped me thus far. Also, I am very fortunate and grateful to honor my father in the Lord, mentor, coach, and pastor, (Dr.) James Fadel, the Continental Overseer of the Redeemed Christian Church of God, the Americas. His counsel and leadership inspired and prepared me for such a time.

Pastor Daniel-Ajayi Adeniran, the Assistant Continental Overseer, the Americas, the Lord knew I would require a pastor as devoted as you, a lover of God's word, and a heart for His flock, guarding the flock against wolves that aim to tear and scatter. I am grateful for your encouragement and support.

I am forever indebted to Dr. Afolabi Aiyedun, pastor of C&S, Staten Island, and national secretary of C&S Churches USA Council, for his encouragement always. He is indeed an outstanding person and an able educator.

Last but not least, I owe so much to my local church, the Redeemed Christian Church of God, International Chapel Queens, Jamaica, New York, for their undying support and their unwavering belief in me, their pastor. I thank you all for your prayers.

INTRODUCTION

This book, *Experiencing God's Glory: The Place, The Situation, and The Time* is divided into two parts. Section 1 includes chapters 1 and 2 that explain the glory of man as it relates to the glory of God and expounds on the revelation of God's nature and attributes. Section 2 includes chapters 3–7, which introduce and elucidate how to experience God's glory in three phases of life and that no matter the challenges in life, there is always glory ahead. The following are the summaries of each chapter:

Section 1

Chapter 1 – "The Glory of Man and the Glory of God": This chapter analyzes how the glory of man emanates from the glory of God.

Chapter 2 – "Beholding the Glory of God": This chapter describes how Jesus is the revelation of the glory of God we behold. This chapter also explains what happens when you behold the glory of God.

Section 2

The second part of this book reveals and explains the stages where we experience the glory of God.

Chapter 3 – "While Waiting to Experience God's Glory": This chapter examines the prerequisites to encounter the glory of God in place, situation, and time.

Chapter 4 – "The Place of Glory": This chapter describes the natural or artificial place where God reveals His greatness, honor, beauty, power, and light to and through us.

Chapter 5 – "Situation of Glory": This chapter expounds on how God can reveal His glory in any circumstance or situation.

Chapter 6 – "The Time of Glory": This chapter explains the time of glory as the revelation of God's glory at God's appointed *perfect* time.

Chapter 7 – "There Is Glory Ahead": This chapter illustrates hope that the future will be better, regardless of the present situation.

SECTION 1

1

The Glory of Man and the Glory of God

The glory of God lives above and beyond any description or definition. To encapsulate the meaning of the glory of God in a statement is unrealistic at best and ineffective at worst. In the article "Doctrine of Glory," Tripp (2018) explains that no single drawing, painting, photograph, or verbal description could ever capture glory. Glory isn't so much a thing as a description of an item. Glory isn't a part of God; it's all

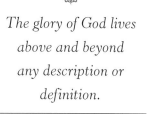

The glory of God lives above and beyond any description or definition.

God is. Every aspect of who God is and every part of what God does is glorious. But even that's not enough of a description. Not only is He glorious in every way, but His very glory is majestic!

One of my favorite movies is *The Lion King*. What interested me most in that movie was the scene where young and curious Simba gets himself (and Nala) into a dangerous situation with the hyenas. The hyenas were prepared to devour Simba, but unknown to Simba, his father, King Mufasa, came to their rescue at the last minute. Simba was afraid and confused prior to the arrival of his father, and he thought he could demonstrate his roaring power to scare off the hyenas. The hyenas were amused and laughed at Simba when he tried to roar the first time. When Simba roared the second time, it was his father's roar that was heard, and the hyenas were scared off. In the context of glory, Simba was unable to reflect the glory of his father until his father was present. Likewise, the glory of humankind reflects God's glory.

To best understand the meaning of the glory of God, it will be expedient to understand the glory of humankind. The first time the word *glory* appears in the Bible is in Genesis 45:13. The scripture revealed the state of Joseph when he was in Egypt. "So you shall tell my father of all my glory in Egypt, and of all that you have seen; and you shall hurry and bring my father down here."

According to John Gill's (2022) *Exposition of the Bible*, the glory of Joseph refers to his God-given wealth and riches, his grandeur and dignity, his power and authority, and other reflections of his wealth, such as the magnificent house in which he dwelled. He had numerous servants, he rode majestically in the second chariot to the king, and he had authority over the people. The people gave him reverence, and he had great power, particularly in the distribution of food. Indeed, all the above described the glory of Joseph. This God-given ability of Joseph affirms the scriptures in Deuteronomy 8:18 that God is the one who gives the power to make wealth. This ability of God described in Proverbs 10:22 explains that such riches like that of Joseph can only be due to blessings from God. From living in his father's house to being sold and taken to Egypt, Joseph eventually became a steward to Potiphar, one of Pharaoh's officials (Genesis 39:1–6). Potiphar's wife tried unsuccessfully to seduce him, and after falsely accusing Joseph, he was imprisoned (Genesis 39:7–20).

Due to his God-given ability to interpret Pharaoh's dream (Genesis 41:16–36), Pharaoh elevated Joseph to the highest official, second only to Pharaoh. He was in charge of administration, security, judgment, and the Pharaoh's safety and the empire (Genesis 41:37–44). He wisely rationed the country's produce in preparation for a time of famine.

Throughout Joseph's life, he enjoyed divine intervention for his glory to be manifested. Joseph affirmed this statement when he reassured his brothers after the death of their father:

> Then his brothers also went and fell down before his face, and they said, "Behold, we are your servants." Joseph said to them, "Do not be afraid, for am I in the Place of God? But as for you, you meant evil against me; but God meant it for good, in order to bring it about as it is this day, to save many people alive. Now therefore, do not be afraid; I will provide for you and your little ones." And he comforted them and spoke kindly to them. (Genesis 50:18–21)

Joseph explained to his brothers that the glory they saw was the result of God's intervention, who made all things work together for him despite all his good and bad experiences (Romans 8:28). In other words, Joseph revealed to his brothers that the purpose of his glory was to reflect God's glory.

The glory of humankind is incomparable to the glory of God. It is rather the reflection of God's glory. Munroe (2001, 78) stated "that the glory of God needs the presence of God to be manifested." Just as a seed needs the soil to bring forth the tree that's trapped inside, so we need the presence of God to bring forth the people, our true selves, that He created us to become, that is, the glory of God. No matter how high our goals or how lofty our dreams are, they will never come to pass until we make the right atmosphere in the presence of God. The scriptures in Genesis 39:2, 21, and 23 reveal that God was with Joseph, hence his reflection of the glory of God in every situation he found himself. However, there is a caveat here; one must be wary of attributing God's glory to oneself. The Bible cautions us in this regard.

Thus says the Lord: "Let not the wise man glory in his wisdom, let not the mighty man glory in his might, Nor let the rich man glory in his riches; But let him who glories Glory in this, That he understands and knows Me, That I am the Lord, exercising lovingkindness, judgment, and righteousness in the earth. For in these I delight," says the Lord. (Jeremiah 9:23–24)

Apostle Paul also reminded his readers that "he who glories, let him glory in the Lord" (2 Corinthians 10:17). To better understand the glory of humankind, these verses have shown, according to Sprout (2001, para. 9), that nothing built for the glory of humankind will survive His scrutiny. But what you do for God's glory will endure forever. So, the sentiment here is that you can attribute glory in two ways.

ATTRIBUTING GLORY TO HUMANKIND

The act of believing that glory belongs to humankind has eaten into the fabric of our lives when in fact our glory only reflects God's glory and does not belong to us. We must not confuse the brilliance of our thoughts, the depth of our spiritual experiences, the consecration of our wills and our ways, and the goodness of our deeds with the wonder of God's Word in our minds (Moore 2014). The story of the people of Shinai in the Bible can expound on attributing glory to humankind. Let me acquaint you with the scriptures.

> Now the whole world had one language and a common speech. As people moved eastward, they found a plain in Shinar and settled there. They said to each other, "Come, let's make bricks and bake them thoroughly." They used brick instead of stone, and tar for mortar. Then they said, "Come, let us build ourselves a city, with a tower that reaches to the heavens, so that we may make a name for ourselves; otherwise we will be scattered over the face of the whole earth." (Genesis 11:1–4)

The above scripture tells the story of the people with deep passion and unity who wanted to build a city and make a name for themselves. In other words, the people planned to build for their glory and not for the glory of God. Babel is not just a biblical story or a fabrication; it is our story; it's like building and making names for ourselves. When we build for our glory, we are going against the Word of God as written in Isaiah 42:8. "I am the Lord, that is My name; And My Glory I will not give to another, Nor My praise to carved images."

God will not share His glory with another because it is immoral for someone to take credit for something they did not do. As a result of their actions in Genesis 11, the greatest and tallest building project humanity ever attempted was resisted by God—and it ended in chaos and confusion.

> But the Lord came down to see the city and the tower the people were building. The Lord said, "If as one people speaking the same language they have begun to do this, then nothing they plan to do will be impossible for them. Come, let us go down and confuse their language so they will not understand each other." So the Lord scattered them from there over all the earth, and they stopped building the

city. That is why it was called Babel—
because there the Lord confused the
language of the whole world. From there
the Lord scattered them over the face of
the whole earth. (Genesis 11:5-9)

The truth is that God created and called His people
to have authority over the earth for His glory, but we
want dominion for the glory of humankind. That's
what was going on at Babel, a distortion, an evil
twisting of the legitimate task that God gave humanity.
There's nothing wrong with building projects. There's
nothing wrong with sowing and reaping. That is our
responsibility from creation, but we must do it under
the authority of God.

Another example I like to enumerate to stress my
view on building for the glory of humankind is in the
book of Daniel.

At the end of twelve months he walked
in the palace of the kingdom of Babylon.
The king spake, and said, Is not this great
Babylon, that I have built for the house of
the kingdom by the might of my power,
and for the honour of my majesty? While

the word was in the King's mouth, there fell a voice from heaven, saying, O king Nebuchadnezzar, to thee it is spoken; The kingdom is departed from thee. And they shall drive thee from men, and thy dwelling shall be with the beasts of the field: they shall make thee to eat grass as oxen, and seven times shall pass over thee, until thou know that the most High ruleth in the kingdom of men, and giveth it to whomsoever he will. The same hour was the thing fulfilled upon Nebuchadnezzar: and he was driven from men, and did eat grass as oxen, and his body was wet with the dew of heaven, till his hairs were grown like eagles' feathers, and his nails like birds' claws. (Daniel 4:29–33)

The verses above reveal how King Nebuchadnezzar was attributing the greatness of Babylon to the might of his power and honor of his majesty to him alone. This notion is contrary to the scriptures. "Give unto the Lord, O you mighty ones, Give unto the Lord glory and strength. Give unto the Lord the Glory due to His name; Worship the Lord in the beauty of holiness" (Psalm 29:1-2).

He was practically giving the praise that is due to God to himself. He had forgotten that he would have been without glory if God were not present, and unless the Lord builds the house, those who labor to build will work in vain, and unless the Lord guards the city, the watchman stays awake in vain (Psalm 127:1-2). We may not be praising ourselves like Nebuchadnezzar, but our actions speak for the same behavior as Nebuchadnezzar.

How many times have you taken credit for how you have been a lifeline for someone? What about pastors taking the glory for growth in the church they planted? This attitude of entitlement to share from God's glory is the main reason the glory of God cannot manifest in many churches today. They have critically left out God, who increases to cause the growth. Paul noted this trend and helped us to understand the process in his letter to the church in Corinth.

> I planted, Apollos watered, but God gave the increase. So then neither he who

plants is anything, nor he who waters, but God who gives the increase. Now he who plants and he who waters are one, and each one will receive his own reward according to his own labor. (1 Corinthians 3:6–8)

We often think that the glory belongs to us. We tend to be lost and forget the source when we are appreciated, honored, and recognized without acknowledging that our glory is only a reflection of God's glory when we are in His presence. That is why in anything we do, we must do to the glory of God. Paul speaks again to the church in Corinth. "But by the grace of God I am what I am: and his grace which was bestowed upon me was not in vain; but I labored more abundantly than they all: yet not I, but the grace of God which was with me" (1 Corinthians 15:10). These scriptures beg the question "Can you become who God wants you to become without the grace of God?"

The other way you can attribute glory is critical in the context of this book, and that is attributing glory to God. We tend to make plans without God, only to call unto Him when we conclude to bless our will. Jesus did not do anything apart from His Father. "Then Jesus answered and said to them, 'Most assuredly, I say to you, the Son can do nothing of Himself, but what He sees the Father do; for whatever He does, the Son also does in like manner'" (John 5:19).

This scripture shows that man can only sustain his glory while in the presence of God. Remember there are people like Nebuchadnezzar and the people of Babel around today. Instead of living for the glory of God, they try to steal that glory for themselves. Instead of living for the glory of God, they try to steal that glory for themselves. Tripp (2018, para. 28) clearly explained this act of stealing.

> He stressed that we demand to be in the center of our world. We take credit for what only God could produce. We want to be sovereign. We want others to worship us. We establish our kingdom and punish those who break our laws. We tell ourselves that we're entitled to what we don't deserve, and we complain when we don't get whatever we want. It's a glory disaster.

Have you attempted to steal glory from God?

Attributing Glory to God

In the opening paragraph of this chapter, I mentioned the movie *The Lion King*. Simba, in the absence of his father, was trying to reflect the splendor, majesty, and honor that belong to his father despite the warning not to leave the palace (his father's presence). Note that he could not manifest the glory due to a lion until his father came to his rescue. Simba is born in the glory of Mufasa; Simba exists in Mufasa's glory; therefore, Simba has a destiny that will eventually manifest the glory of his father. Let's bring this scene into our lives.

- God created us in His glory—the source of our glory.

  > Everyone who is called by My name,
  > Whom I have created for My glory;
  > I have formed him, yes, I have made
  > him. (Isaiah 43:7)

- We exist in His glory. Ready to bring Him glory, we are a living sacrifice.

  > For we are His workmanship, created
  > in Christ Jesus for good works, which

God prepared beforehand that we should walk in them. (Ephesians 2:10)

- We must manifest His glory. In other words, there must be a performance to manifest the glory of God in our lives.

    This people I have formed for Myself; They shall declare My praise. (Isaiah 43:21)

    Let your light so shine before men, that they may see your good works and glorify your Father in heaven. (Matthew 5:16)

The presence of God is vital for humans to manifest the glory of God successfully. In other words, all glory belongs to God, and you cannot separate His glory from Him. Otherwise, it will fade. Jesus reinforces this explanation in his own life. "I can of Myself do nothing. As I hear, I judge; and My judgment is righteous, because I do not seek My own will but the will of the Father who sent Me" (John 5:30). Jesus is the glory of God in the natural dimension for our benefit,

> who being the brightness of His Glory and the express image of His Person, and upholding all things by the word of His power, when He had by Himself purged our sins, sat down at the right hand of the majesty on high. (Hebrews 1:3)

And when we are in the presence of the Lord, we go, or we are transformed "from glory to glory" (2 Corinthians 3:18). The glory of God is the invisible qualities, character, or attributes of God displayed in a visible (or knowable) way. The glory of God is His invisible character made visible (Ballenger, 2022). The glory of God is the invisible made visible through looking at Jesus Christ. Jesus glorifies God more than any other because he reveals God more than any other (God made flesh). Today, we see something of God's glory by faith as we trust in Jesus. One day we will see this glory in its most total sense. On that day, we will view Christ by sight and not merely by faith. But that does not mean we are unable to gain a true glimpse of God's glory now as we look to Christ. And as we grow in our knowledge of Christ, we will also grow in our longing to see the fullness of the divine glory (Ligonier, 2017, para. 5).

All glory belongs to God. Therefore, we must attribute all glory to God. The Bible stated clearly in 1 Corinthians 1:31, "He who glories let him glory in the Lord."

We need to learn two lessons from this verse. First, we need to attribute glory to God, and second, we must acknowledge that our glory would not be possible without Him. These lessons support my previous analysis that the glory of humans is a reflection of God's glory in His presence. God wants the spotlight on Him. Therefore, everything that God does is to give Him glory! "He must increase, but I must decrease" (John 3:31), says John the Baptist, because it is all about God and not about you. He does not share His glory (Isaiah 42:8).

- God created the universe to declare His glory.

    The heavens declare the glory of God; And the firmament shows His handiwork. (Psalm 19:1)

- God chose created and chose you to His glory.

  Even every one that is called by my
  name: for I have created him for my
  glory, I have formed him; yea, I have
  made him. (Isaiah 43:7)

- God allows troubles in our life so, in the end, we
  can glorify Him.

  And call upon me in the day of
  trouble: I will deliver thee, and thou
  shalt glorify me. (Psalm 50:15)

- Ultimately, God sent Jesus to earth to glorify
  Him through the assignment given to him.

  I have glorified You on the earth. I
  have finished the work which You
  have given Me to do. (John 17:4)

You cannot give glory to God unless you know
Him, and the only way to know Him is through the
Gospel of Jesus Christ, which displays the glory of God
superlatively. Paul wrote,

For we do not preach ourselves, but
Christ Jesus the Lord, and ourselves your
bondservants for Jesus' sake. For it is the
God who commanded light to shine out
of darkness, who has shone in our hearts
to give the light of the knowledge of the
glory of God in the face of Jesus Christ.
(2 Corinthians 4:5–6)

The apostle Paul reiterates the Gospel as the means
by which God wants us to know the riches and the
glory of Christ. "To them God willed to make known
what are the riches of the Glory of this mystery among
the Gentiles: which is Christ in you, the hope of Glory"
(Colossians 1:27).

The final objective of Jesus's sacrifice was to restore
human beings to the realm of God's glory, for which
God created us so that we can fulfill that scripture in
our text today.

But we all, with unveiled face, beholding
as in a mirror the glory of the Lord, are
being transformed into the same image
from glory to glory, just as by the Spirit
of the Lord. (2 Corinthians 3:18)

There's nothing wrong with success, greatness, building, innovation, or creating. There's nothing wrong with sowing and reaping. Those are the tasks God gave to us in creation, and we are to do them, *coram Deo*, before the face of God, under the authority of God, and unto the glory of God (in the presence of God).

2

BEHOLDING THE GLORY OF GOD

The ultimate goal of being something is to be influenced by it or reflect on the experience. The verb *behold*, as defined in the *Oxford English Dictionary*, means "to see or observe someone or something, especially of remarkable or impressive nature." Our hearts are engaged when we behold something, and our affections get stimulated as we admire what we perceive to be remarkable or impressive. Piper (2021, para. 2) states,

We become like what we watch in one of his teachings. The objects of our attention shape our becoming. Our potential as creatures is realized by what we behold. We are moldable clay creatures, conforming to whatever most attracts our gaze. What we behold shapes us, for better or for worse.

For example, God showed Abraham how numerous his descendants would be. "Then He brought him outside and said, 'Look now toward heaven, and count the stars if you are able to number them.' And He said to him, 'So shall your descendants be'" (Genesis 15:5–6).

Abraham was inspired and assured by what God showed him. He was transformed by what he beheld, and ultimately, he had Isaac at an impossible age of one hundred years old while his wife, Sarah, was ninety years old.

The Lord was gracious to Sarah as he had said, and the Lord did for Sarah what he had promised. Sarah became pregnant and bore a son to Abraham in his old age, at the very time God had promised him. Abraham gave the name Isaac to the son Sarah bore him. (Genesis 21:1–3)

Beholding the glory of God infers seeing the revelation of God's nature and attributes. And as we established in the previous chapter, by substitution, beholding the glory of God means beholding Jesus Christ because Jesus is the revelation of the glory of God. Before we consider Jesus as the revelation of the glory of God, it's essential first to ask this: what is the glory of God? The glory of God is the shining forth of who He is. It's the manifestation of His Person. Jesus reveals the nature and character of God. According to Hebrews 1:3, Jesus is the exact imprint of the nature of God. We see the glory of God in Jesus because Jesus perfectly reveals the nature and character of God. "He is the image of the invisible God, the firstborn over all creation … For it pleased the Father that in Him all the fullness should dwell" (Colossians 1:15, 19).

As previously mentioned, Jesus makes the invisible God visible. The Gospel of John revealed that in Jesus, the invisible God is made visible. While no one has ever seen God, in Jesus He is revealed.

> No one has seen God at any time. The only begotten Son, who is in the bosom of the Father, He has declared Him. (John 1:18)

While no one has seen the Father, Jesus makes Him known.

> Philip said to Him, "Lord, show us the Father, and it is sufficient for us." Jesus said to him, "Have I been with you so long, and yet you have not known Me, Philip? He who has seen Me has seen the Father; so how can you say, 'Show us the Father'? (John 14:7–9)

To behold the glory of God, we must make an effort to see Jesus as the revelation of the glory of God because it is the prerequisite for transformation from glory to glory. Apostle Paul explained, "But we all, with unveiled face, beholding as in a mirror the glory of the Lord, are being transformed into the

To behold the glory of God, we must make an effort to see Jesus as the revelation of the glory of God

same image from glory to glory, just as by the Spirit of the Lord" (2 Corinthians 3:18).

As Paul wrote, we must be able to see (unveiled) to continually behold the glory of our Lord Jesus Christ for transformation in his likeness to occur in our lives. In his article "The Four Dimensions of Experiencing the Holy Spirit," Fadel (2022, para. 7) bolsters Paul's claim that "when you behold the word and engage in it, immersing yourself in the Spirit and life in the word of God, you will move from glory to glory." We can benefit from beholding Jesus as the revelation of the glory of God. The following paragraphs explain five things that can happen when we behold Jesus as the revelation of the glory of God.

It Is an Opportunity for Us to Know God

There is a difference between when a person knows me directly and when a person knows me through my friend or brother. The person who knows me directly knows more about me than the person who knows me through another friend. With this understanding, we have the opportunity to know God when we behold

Jesus as the revelation of the fullness of God. We can see in Jesus the character of God on display because Jesus is God in the flesh. The apostle Paul says that, although Jesus was "in very nature God, He did not consider equality with God something to be used to his own advantage; rather, he made himself nothing by taking the very nature of a servant, being made in human likeness" (Philippians 2:6–7). In his letter to the Colossians, he said, "In Christ lives all the fullness of God in a human body" (Colossians 2:9). Apart from knowing God through Jesus Christ, Jesus also made it possible for us to come to the presence of God because He was the ultimate and flawless sacrifice that forever satisfied God's wrath against sin (Hebrews 10:14). His divine nature made Him fit for the work of Redeemer; His human body allowed Him to shed the blood necessary to redeem, a debt that no one with a sinful nature could pay (Matthew 26:28). No one else could meet the requirements to become the sacrifice for the whole world's sins (1 John 2:2).

Summarily, Jesus wanted the people at Lazarus's tomb to know God while they beheld him. This demonstration was evident in his prayer. "And I know that You always hear Me, but because of the people who are standing by I said this, that they may believe that You sent Me" (John 11:42).

IT GIVES ASSURANCE THAT WE ARE INDEED CHILDREN OF GOD

Christ is the assurance of our salvation. God speaks of the assurance people have when they look to Jesus.

> Can a woman forget her nursing child, And not have compassion on the son of her womb? Surely they may forget Yet I will not forget you, See, I have inscribed you on the palms of My hands; Your walls are continually before Me. (Isaiah 49:15–16)

He gave us the right to become children of God when we receive Him and believe in His name through the Gospel (John 1:12). Your faith in Jesus Christ also confirms you are all sons of God (Galatians 3:26). Apostle Paul elucidates in 2 Corinthians 4:3–6 that children of God are those who have the knowledge of the glory of God in the face of Jesus Christ. They see God's glory in Jesus and respond in repentance, obedience, and worship. But those who don't believe in Jesus don't see Him as glorious because they are blind, don't submit to Him as Lord, and don't worship Him as God. It's never too late. If you can behold, love, and submit to the glory of God in Jesus, you can have the assurance that you are indeed a child of God's love.

WE BECOME LIKE JESUS CHRIST

The most intriguing thing that could happen when we behold Jesus is that transformation to His likeness is inevitable. Again, Apostle Paul wrote,

> But even to this day, when Moses is read, a veil lies on their heart. Nevertheless when one turns to the Lord, the veil is taken away. Now the Lord is the spirit; and where the Spirit of the Lord is, there is liberty. But we all, with unveiled face, beholding as in a mirror the Glory of the Lord, are being transformed into the same image from Glory to Glory, just as by the Spirit of the Lord. (2 Corinthians 3:15–18)

We become and understand better what we behold. The children become what they see in their parents. That is why the scriptures advise parents to train their children in the way they should go, and when they are old, they will not depart from the training (Proverbs 22:6). There is a difference between the verb *teach* and *train*. The terms *teaching* and *training* come up often interchangeably, but there are important distinctions. Teaching provides knowledge, instruction, or information, while training develops abilities through practice with instruction or supervision. The verb *train* is preferred because children behold and imitate what they become in their parents through examples over time. Likewise, the apostle Paul observed that as we behold the glory of the Lord over time, we are transformed into the image of Christ with the help of the Holy Spirit. Paul again says we should follow his examples as he follows the model of Christ (1 Corinthians 11:1). As we behold Christ, He will train us in the way we should go with the help of the Holy Spirit until we become like Him.

Our Relationship with the Lord Changes

In Isaiah's vision, he saw the Lord sitting on a throne, high and lifted up, and the train of His robe filled the temple (Isaiah 6:1) (i.e., God's glory). He realized some things were wrong with him in his relationship with God. Isaiah, until that encounter, strayed away from Him. He had been out of fellowship with God. Here is what Isaiah said in that vision when the glory of God revealed to him his identity: "Woe is me, for I am undone! Because I am a man of unclean lips, And I dwell in the midst of a people of unclean lips; For my eyes have seen the King, The Lord of hosts" (Isaiah 5:5).

Also, after Saul encountered Jesus on the way to Damascus to persecute men and women who were followers of Jesus, we see a change in his life. He was in deep fellowship with God. Here is how apostle Paul refers to himself:

> For you have heard of my former conduct in Judaism, how I persecuted the Church of God beyond measure and tried to destroy it. And I advanced in Judaism

beyond many of my contemporaries in my own nation, being more exceedingly zealous for the traditions of my fathers. But when it pleased God, who separated me from my mother's womb and called me through His grace, to reveal His Son in me, that I might preach Him among the Gentiles, I did not immediately confer with flesh and blood, nor did I go up to Jerusalem to those who were apostles before me; but I went to Arabia, and returned again to Damascus. (Galatians 1:13–17)

The above scriptures describe how Paul turned from a dreadful persecutor of followers of Jesus to one who had a passion for spreading the gospel in cities and nations. This effect of seeing God's glory brings to focus my fifth point. That is, when we behold Jesus as a reflection of the glory of God, it is impossible to remain the same or continue to do the same things before the encounter. Instead, our passion for the lost soul will increase without bounds. Our love for God and the things of God now take priority in our lives.

And we begin to live for Jesus Christ even if it costs us our lives (Philippians 1:21).

WE SUBMIT VOLUNTARILY FOR HIS ASSIGNMENTS

When we have seen the glory of God in Jesus, we become desperate to work for Him no matter how uncomfortable or impossible the task might be. It is now different from when we used to be our own boss. At that time, we approved and disapproved at will, but when we behold Jesus, we become a living sacrifice and will to do anything or go anywhere God wants us to do or go. This voluntary submission comes naturally with zeal to be ready for any responsibility God may have for us. Look at the example of Isaiah again. After he saw the glory of God, he became genuinely available wherever God wanted to send him. "God said to Isaiah, 'Whom shall I send, and who will go for us?' and Isaiah replied, 'Here I am! Send me'" (Isaiah 6:7–9).

So the big question is whether Isaiah was on an errand for himself or God before he saw God's glory. Here's Saul's conversation during his encounter with Jesus:

He said, "Who are You, Lord?" Then the Lord said, "I am Jesus, whom you are persecuting. It is hard for you to kick against the goads." So he, trembling and astonished, said, "Lord, what do You want me to do?" Then the Lord said to him, "Arise and go into the city, and you will be told what you must do." (Acts 9:5–6)

Many of us are working for our glory, and only an encounter with Jesus can reveal this anomaly to us. When we submit to Jesus, He will work through us, and we will begin to work in His might. In Piper's (2022, para. 26) conviction, God gets the glory, not from our heroic exertion but our reliance upon his strength. Apostle Paul stated that he could do all things through Christ, who gives him strength (Philippians 4:13). He also acknowledged that God works in you to will and act to fulfill His good purpose (Philippians 2:13). The question now is this: how do I behold as the revelation of the glory of God? In the following few paragraphs, we shall be learning the answers.

SECTION 2

3

WHILE WAITING TO EXPERIENCE GOD'S GLORY

This chapter introduces how in waiting, you can experience the glory of God in three phases: *place*, *situation*, and *time*, to be discussed in detail in the following three chapters. Isaiah projects how these phases in our lives can reveal the glory of God,

> But now, thus says the Lord, who created
> you, O Jacob, And He who formed you,
> O Israel: "Fear not, for I have redeemed
> you; I have called you by your name; You
> are Mine. When you pass through the

waters, I will be with you; And through the rivers, they shall not overflow you. When you walk through the fire, you shall not be burned, Nor shall the flame scorch you." (Isaiah 43:1–2).

In the above scriptures, *adverse situations* can occur in our lives, "overflowing with water and burning in fire," like being buried in precarious conditions. There are strange places where you can find yourself in "the river and the fire," like places where you are helpless and cannot navigate. God reveals His glory for you to see when He brings you through the fire of life instead of saving you from it; therefore, you can be rest assured when you find yourself in the fire of life predicaments like sickness, divorce, or financial ruin.

So in this story, we can see how the combination of place, situation, and time revealed the glory of God. To experience the glory of God in His ordained *place*, *situation*, and *time* for us, certain practices must be in place to keep you in check and prepare you. I refer to these attitudes as "practice in waiting to experience God's glory."

Believe His Word

When you put your absolute trust in His word, you will see the glory of God. Jesus demonstrated how the glory of God could be revealed to us when we believe Him when He raised Lazarus from the dead. "Jesus said to her, 'Did I not say to you that if you would believe you would see the glory of God?'" (John 11:40). It was difficult for Mary and Martha to believe that Jesus would raise Lazarus in such a hopeless situation. Jesus's assuring Martha said, "I am the resurrection and the life. He who believes in Me, though he may die, he shall live. And whoever lives and believes in Me shall never die. Do you believe this?" (John 11:25–26). Martha responded, "Yes, Lord, I believe that You are the Christ, the Son of God, who is to come into the world" (John 11:27).

Martha's belief was enough to reveal the glory of God. Trust God even though things don't make complete sense to you now. When it's difficult to believe, at least confess Christ, and you will see the glory of God on display. No obstacle is too big for God to turn around for you and His glory. The miracle is about the revelation or manifestation of God's attributes or excellences. Here we see the wonder of what He can do. In the commentary on John 11:40, Grant (2017, para. 8) stated,

> Jesus did not use pomp and circumstance to call attention to the miracle. The fact that the miracle was all people were expecting, the raising of Lazarus from the dead was a spectacular miracle from Jesus; however, He did not emphasize the miracle but the Glory of God. We need to focus on God's Glory in our lives. This incident is the true significance of what life is. It is not whether you are worthy to see it. Faith opens us to the reality of what God has to offer us. You can see His Glory by faith. The miracle did not depend on Martha's faith; it depended solely on Jesus Himself.

Therefore, you must believe in God's word because He is the beginning and the end. He knows the finish from the start. He has the final say; even death does not have the final say. As I like to put it, He is the producer, and the production goes according to His plan. Allow God, and let your situation reveal the glory of God.

Praise God Continually

A psalm of David says, "I will bless the Lord at all times; His praise shall continually be in my mouth" (Psalm 34:1). Another psalm says, "Let my mouth be filled with Your praise And with Your glory all the day" (Psalm 71:8).

The meaning of "all the day" suggests good times, bad times of the day, days of adversity, and windfall. When King Solomon dedicated the temple, there were a massive choir and 120 trumpets and other instruments. The choir sang, "The Lord is good; His love endures forever" (2 Chronicles 5:13). We read that "the glory of the Lord filled the temple" (v. 14).

God's glory came down in prison through intense prayer and praise rendered by Paul and Silas. This Bible story begins with the unjust arrest of Paul and Silas. Because they had cast a spirit of divination out of a girl, the local Philippian authorities beat them and then threw them into a jail cell. Besides the trauma of the severe beating, they fasten their arms and legs in an immobile position (Acts 16:16–24). Instead of being engrossed in self-pity, they sang high praises to God, worshipping Him for counting them worthy to experience the fellowship of Christ's suffering. The result was shaking the prison to its foundations and losing the chains with which they were bound (Acts 16:25–26). The Bible says that God inhabits in the praises of His people (Psalm 22:3). In other words, God *dwells* in the atmosphere of His praise. Praise to God is a vehicle of faith that takes us into His presence and power. In the article "The Power of Praise & Worship," Robbins (2022, para. 6) states, "Praise and worship is the *gate-pass* which allows us to enter the sacredness of His glory." The psalmist writes, "Enter into his gates with thanksgiving, and into his courts with praise: be thankful unto him, and bless his name" *(Psalm 100:4).* Paul and Silas knew the secret of how to lift their hearts above their troubles and enter God's presence and power. Through praise and worship, their hearts were raised into God's joyous presence and peace and provided God a channel for His power to operate in their circumstances.

Pray Always

The apostle Paul emphasized the importance of prayer to the church in Thessalonica when he urges them to pray without ceasing (1 Thessalonians 5:17). We can see and experience the glory of God when we diligently ask and seek for it. Jesus Christ demonstrated how to pray in order to see the glory of God. He prayed that people standing by Lazarus's tomb might believe so they could see the glory of God (John 11:41–42). The people standing by were expecting a miracle; however, Jesus did not emphasize the miracle but the glory of God. We must keep the focus on the glory of God in our lives because His glory precedes manifest the miracles that meet our needs. Experiencing God's glory through prayer is displayed when the glory appeared in the upper room on the Day of Pentecost and sat on each person's head there (Acts 2:1–4). So how do you pray for the glory of God?

- Pray for God to reveal His glory *to* you. That was Moses's prayer. "Please, show me Your glory" (Exodus 33:18).
- Pray for God to reveal His glory *in* you. "For I consider the sufferings of this present time

are not worthy to be compared with the glory which shall be revealed in us" (Romans 8:18).

When we pray for the manifestation of the glory of God, miracles, signs, and wonders will occur in the church, communities, and our personal lives. Therefore, seek God to glorify His name in all you do, and miracles will follow.

BE HOLY SPIRIT FILLED

To be filled with the Holy Spirit means to be wholly controlled by the Holy Spirit. It means that the Holy Spirit has the freedom to occupy every part of our lives, guiding and controlling us. Being Spirit filled is centered upon a continual process of spiritual growth and maturity that can only be found and cultivated by the Spirit of God. As we walk with the Lord, this is a daily submission, being filled for His glory. "And do not be drunk with wine, in which is dissipation; but be filled with the Spirit" (Ephesians 5:18).

We need continual infilling of the Holy Spirit and a close walk with the Lord to see God's glory. The Holy Spirit also empowers us to always do God's work in God's presence, thus experiencing His glory.

Stephen was filled with the Holy Spirit, and he boldly and rightly rebuked the nation of Israel of failing to recognize Jesus as their Messiah, rejecting and murdering Him (Acts 7:55–56). He reminded them how they had murdered Zechariah and other prophets and faithful men throughout their generations. The council members were furious, and just before they stoned him, he saw the glory of God.

> When they heard these things they were cut to the heart, and they gnashed at him with their teeth. But he, being full of the Holy Spirit, gazed into heaven and saw the Glory of God, and Jesus standing at the right hand of God, and said, Look! I see the heavens opened and the Son of Man standing at the right hand of God! (Acts 7:54–56).

Stephen saw the glory of God as he was propagating the gospel under the influence of the Holy Spirit. Therefore, you must pause and ask yourself why you are not experiencing God's glory in your life and ministry.

Share the Good News

When the Holy Spirit brings sinners to experience salvation in the new birth, He reveals this glory of God in the person. "For God, who said, "Let there be light in the darkness," has made this light shine in our hearts so we could know the Glory of God that is seen in the face of Jesus Christ" (2 Corinthians 4:6).

The good news concerning Christ and the way of salvation is the light that shines in the darkness to reveal the glory of God, as seen in the example of Stephen. When we look at the scriptures from Genesis to Revelation, it is evident that God uniquely reveals His glory, sometimes at an unusual or usual place, sometimes in an adverse or favorable situation, and sometimes when it is least expected. In the following chapters of this book, I believe the experiences will encourage you to look ahead to the glory of God. No matter what the obstacles might be, they will always make way for the glory of God to manifest.

No matter what the obstacles might be, they will always make way for the glory of God to manifest.

4

THE PLACE OF GLORY

In the article "The 5 Themes of Geography," Rosenberg (2019, para. 3) describes a *place* as "the human and physical characteristics of a location." Physical features of a place may include a description of mountains, rivers, beaches, topography, climate, and animal and plant life. The human characteristics of a place may consist of human-designed cultural features. These features include land use, architectural styles, forms of livelihood, religious practices, political systems, common foods, means of transportation, and methods of communication. From Rosenberg's description, one can deduce that a place can exist naturally or occur in human terms from the above definitions. On this premise, the *Place of Glory* describes the natural or man-ascribed place where God reveals His greatness, honor, beauty, power, and light to and through His people. It does not matter whether the place exists naturally or in our day-to-day activities. God can reveal His glory anywhere, and nothing can stop Him. Bringing to focus the story of the three Hebrew boys, the fire could not stop the revelation of the glory of God to deliver the Hebrew boys

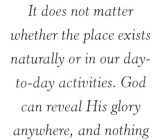

It does not matter whether the place exists naturally or in our day-to-day activities. God can reveal His glory anywhere, and nothing can stop Him.

(Daniel 3). It does not matter where you are in the storm of life; God will always reveal His glory to save you and glorify His name.

GLORY AT A LOWLY PLACE

It is not uncommon for God to reveal His glory in the lowly and humblest places; therefore, you can experience the glory of God in a lowly place. Let us examine glory at a lowly place from the perspective of a place like a manger. The manger, where farmers keep their animals, was the least likely birthplace for Jesus Christ. Piper (2017, para. 7) summarizes, "The first bed for the Son of God was not a royal cradle. It was a common corn crib." God's Son deserved a high-profile birth in the most elegant of surroundings. But instead, God's Son made His appearance on earth in the lowliest circumstances. Jesus was born in humility, and He was, and He is still approachable, accessible, and available. No palace gates hinder the way to Him or have guards to prevent our approach. The King of kings came humbly, and His first bed was a manger. The place of birth of Jesus Christ reveals that sometimes the lowliest, messiest, dirtiest, most broken, and most imperfect places are where you see God's glory penetrate most powerfully and beautifully. The surprises of life are places you see God's glory shine most brightly, and of all places on earth, *His glory shines in a manger, not in a palace.*

> "And this will be the sign to you: You will find a Babe wrapped in swaddling clothes, lying in a manger." And suddenly there was with the angel a multitude

of the heavenly host praising God and saying: "Glory to God in the highest, And on earth peace, goodwill toward men!" (Luke 2:12–14)

God revealed His glory in the manger. So you can also experience the glory of God in your life wherever you are, no matter how lowly, messy, dirty, and imperfect the place might be, just as the three wise men did experience the glory of God in the manger (Matthew 2:1–12).

GLORY AT THE TOMB

The deadness of a place such as a tomb cannot stop the revelation of the glory of God. A tomb is a place of interment or an area beneath the ground for the burial of a corpse. However, even the tomb could not stop the glory of God from being revealed. The scriptures from John 11 narrate how Lazarus became sick and died and how Jesus raised him from the dead to the glory of God.

When Jesus, again groaning in Himself, came to the tomb. It was a cave, and a stone lay against it. Jesus said, "Take away the stone." Martha, the sister of him who was dead, said to Him, "Lord, by this time there is a stench, for he has been dead four days." Jesus said to her, "Did I not say to you that if you would believe you would see the glory of God?" Then they took away the stone from the place where the dead man was lying. And Jesus lifted up His eyes and said, "Father, I thank You that You have heard Me. And I know that You always hear Me, but because of the people who are standing by I said this, that they may believe that You sent Me." Now when He had said these things, He cried with a loud voice, "Lazarus, come forth!" And he who had died came out bound hand and foot with graveclothes, and his face was wrapped with a cloth. Jesus said to them, "Loose him, and let him go." (John 11:37–44)

God can reveal His glory to and through us in a hopeless place like the Lazarus tomb. Lazarus's tomb was a place of death, crying, sorrow, and pain. Yet at this rare place, Jesus chose to reveal the glory of God to the people standing by. The revelation of God's glory at the tomb of Lazarus evidenced that God can reveal His glory to and through us at any place.

GLORY AT THE FIREPLACE

In their captivity, the story of the three Hebrew young men, Shadrach, Meshach, and Abednego, known initially as Hananiah, Mishael, and Azariah, respectively (Daniel 1:6–7), illustrates how a place, situation, and time revealed the glory of God. It is critical to note here that these three Hebrew boys learned the ways of their God at home in Israel then continued with their capture into slavery by King Nebuchadnezzar of Babylon. In captivity, the Babylonians forced these boys to learn their ways. A time of test came when Nebuchadnezzar ordered that whenever his musicians played their instruments, all men must bow down to a giant golden image of the king. They chose to face death instead of dishonoring the God of their youth. Even in captivity, everything was going well with them until a time they did not envision came when they had to worship an idol. I believe they allowed the word of the second of the Ten Commandments to guide them in their decision-making. "You shall have no other gods before me" (Exodus 20:2).

The time that will reveal the glory of God is a time of distress that also requires perseverance and faithfulness. Perseverance is vital to growing in your faith. God wants His people to persevere no matter what happens, so we have to learn how to overcome obstacles, difficulties, trials, and tribulations to experience victory in Christ. God has so much more in store for us, and His plan is such that struggles and hardships become blessings and rewards if we persevere to His glory. King Nebuchadnezzar was so furious that he ordered his servants to throw the three young men into a fiery furnace. But to the king's absolute disbelief, the boys were not burned but are seen walking among the flames. Here are the words of King Nebuchadnezzar exclaiming what he saw: "Look! I see four men walking around in the fire, unbound and unharmed, and the fourth looks like a son of the gods" (Daniel 3:25).

God saved them from the fire. He revealed His

glory through Jesus Christ as He walked with them through the fire. The place of fire cannot stop the revelation of the glory of God for your deliverance. So always remember you are not alone in the place of fire. It's a matter of divine timing that God will reveal His glory to deliver you.

Are you in a place of hopelessness like Lazarus or in the fire like the three Hebrew boys? Are you in an area that is not of choice, or are you helpless where you are? I want to assure you that irrespective of where you are today, God knows about it and it is for Him to reveal His glory in you and through you for others to see. The nature of your location cannot prevent the revelation of God's glory.

GLORY AT LODEBAR

The deadness of a place such as Lodebar cannot stop the revelation of the glory of God. *Lodebar* in Hebrew means a place of no pasture, and it was a town of forgotten people, including Mephibosheth. Mephibosheth was the son of Jonathan, the grandson of King Saul. Jonathan was a special friend of King David. In the likes of Lodebar, you would find the lost, unskilled, and uneducated outcasts from society—those whom people would scorn, those whom we would pass by and pay no attention to, and those who would be just another statistic on a government report.

After taking the throne through God's will, King David asked if there were any other relatives of Saul, the previous king who, in jealousy, had tried to murder David. David wanted to show Saul's family kindness because of his friendship with Saul's son, Jonathan, who had died during a war. Jonathan had a son who was crippled and living in hiding at Lodebar because he was afraid that David would kill him because of what King Saul did to David. It was common for a new king to kill the rest of the royal family in those days, so there was no threat to the throne. David sent for Mephibosheth, Johnathan's son, so he could "show the kindness of God to him" (2 Samuel 9:3). When Mephibosheth came to David, he was expecting to be killed and fell on his face and paid homage to him. David responded, "Do not fear, for I will show you kindness for the sake of your father Johnathan and I will restore to you all the land of Saul your father and you shall eat at my table always" (2 Samuel 9:7). This story seems small and short when in reality it is full of love and a reflection of God's love. David's promise and show of kindness to Johnathan's son depicts how God reveals His glory through kindness to save humanity.

> But when the kindness and the love of God our Savior toward man appeared, not by works of righteousness which we have done, but according to His mercy He saved us, through the washing of regeneration and renewing of the Holy Spirit. (Titus 3:4–5)

Sometimes, you are like Mephibosheth in Lodebar, but the revelation of God's glory through His kindness, love, and grace toward you will surely bring you out to a place of glory.

From Lodebar to the palace, a tremendous difference in place and only the glory of God in His kindness can bring about such relocation from hopelessness to a place of hope. The physical or the spiritual nature of where you are now cannot and will not stop the revelation of the glory of God from relocating you. God's revealed glory will bring you out whether you are in a wilderness, isolation, desolation, or lack.

GLORY AT THE PLACE OF CAPTIVITY

The revelation of the glory of God is practical in a place of captivity like the prison. This revelation can be appreciated in the case of Paul and Silas when they encountered a slave woman possessed by the spirit of divination (Acts 16:16), and Paul cast the demon out of her in Jesus's name (Acts 16:18). This performance angered her masters because they feared they would not be able to earn money from her anymore. Then they brought the two apostles to the marketplace, where they faced the high magistrates (Acts 16:19–20). Paul and Silas were apprehended and whipped. Following the beating, they were locked up and chained to stocks. While in prison, they prayed and sang praises unto God at midnight, and the prisoners heard them (Acts 16:21–25). Suddenly, a great earthquake shook the prison's foundations, immediately causing all the doors to open and everyone's chains to become loose. The prison guard, fearing for his life for failing to stop the two men from escaping, wanted to kill himself rather than face the possibility of torture or execution. But Paul called out to him and told him not to hurt himself. After the chaos, he shared the Word of the

Lord with him, and the guard found salvation to the glory of God (Acts 16:26–36).

It did not matter whether the magistrates were justified or not to put Paul and Silas in jail; what mattered was that God used Paul and Silas to reveal His glory. The Bible in Isaiah further complements this narrative.

> Shall the prey be taken from the mighty, Or the captives of the righteous be delivered? But thus says the Lord: "Even the captives of the mighty shall be taken away, And the prey of the terrible be delivered; For I will contend with him who contends with you, And I will save your children." (Isaiah 49:24–25)

The experience of Paul and Silas still holds today. Although your location might be limiting you and you may be experiencing delays due to where you are now, pray and praise God, and He will reveal His glory in and through you to set you free from the place of captivity.

5

SITUATION REVEALING THE GLORY OF GOD

God can reveal His glory in any circumstances or situation. In other words, there is no situation that is too dire for God to reveal His glory, and there is no situation that is too splendid for the revelation of God's glory to surpass. Do you feel you are in a prison situation, trapped in sin, or burdened with grief that you feel helpless or paralyzed by suffering or a

There is no situation that is too dire for God to reveal His glory, and there is no situation that is too splendid for the revelation of God's glory to surpass.

fear of the future or lack of desire for Christ and his truth? When we feel overcome by the weight of our circumstances and the battle seems to be more than we can bear, we can wait, watch, and trust in the saving power of God's glory. The following scriptures show us how to trust the Lord for the revelation of His glory in distress:

> In my distress I called upon the Lord, And cried out to my God; He heard my voice from His temple, And my cry came before Him, even to His ears. (Psalm 18:6)

> He sent from above, He took me; He drew me out of many waters. He delivered me from my strong enemy, From those who hated me, For they were too strong for me. They confronted me in the day of my calamity, But the Lord was my support. He also brought me out into a broad place; He delivered me because He delighted in me. (Psalm 18:16–19)

In every situation, God can reveal His glory to deliver you so you can fulfill His plan for you and give Him all the glory. I will share some situations in which the power of God's glory can deliver.

A Situation That Appears as if Evil Is Winning

In the summary account of Peter's imprisonment in Acts 12:1–17, King Herod (king of the Jewish people) persecuted Christians and ordered the arrest of the apostle Peter. The whole church was very afraid, so they gathered in a house to pray. While praying, an angel visited Peter's prison cell and miraculously released him. Peter found his way to the place where the church was praying. Peter later went into hiding, but Herod was eventually struck down by an angel when he received praise from the people as if he were God. At first glance, it would seem that Peter's imprisonment was getting in the way of the work Christ had given him. However, the power of God's glory revealed by an angel changed the situation to deliver Peter from the prison situation and avert the devil's destructive attempts.

Occasionally, circumstances that may seem like a hindrance to the propagation of the gospel and a threat to our lives may be the very springboard God uses to display the gospel through us. As Christians, we can be confident that even circumstances that perplex us are divinely arranged to grow us up in Christ and reveal His glory. Evil may appear to flourish for a time, but the power of God's glory will ultimately prevail. "When the wicked spring up like grass, And when all the workers of iniquity flourish, it is that they may be destroyed forever" (Psalm 92:7).

With God on your side, there is no way evil can have the last say or laugh over your situation. It may only seem like evil is winning, but the revelation of the glory of God will give you the opportunity of the last say and laugh over your frightful circumstance. The scripture warns those who are rejoicing over you because they thought they are gaining over you. "Do not rejoice over me, my enemy; When I fall, I will arise; When I sit in darkness, The Lord will be a light to me" (Micah 7:8).

GLORY FROM TRIALS

Another way to experience the revelation of God's glory for your deliverance is through your pain, trials, discomfort, or challenges. Your pain, your emotions, and your story are not for naught. Behind these circumstances, God has glory waiting to be unveiled. He has power waiting to be revealed. He has encouragement awaiting your soul. Here are the wise words of James:

> My brethren, count it all joy when you fall into various trials, knowing that the testing of your faith produces patience. But let patience have its perfect work, that you may be [b]perfect and complete, lacking nothing ... Blessed is the man who endures temptation; for when he has been approved, he will receive the crown of life which the Lord has promised to those who love Him. (James 1:2–4; 12)

God stands ready to show you how to see God's glory hidden in your present-day circumstances. In his book *The Purpose and Power of God's Glory*, Munroe (2001) explained that pressure is one of the keys to releasing the glory of God in us. If we never faced any challenges, we would never grow. How would we ever learn that God can solve problems if we never had any problems? Pressure situations teach us to depend on God because they quickly drive us to outspend our resources. When we reach the "end of our rope," God is there, ready and waiting to deal with the situation and bring out His glory in us. What we see as problems God sees as opportunities to manifest His glory. Our challenge is to learn how to stop looking at our circumstances through our own eyes and start seeing them from God's perspective. Circumstances are God's gifts to our glory. God brings us into certain circumstances because He wants to show Himself off in our lives. He wants us to expose the glory within us and often uses life situations to help us. Whatever God allows to challenge us is to bring out what is inside us. The problems we face are real opportunities for us to show the world who we really are: children of God and overcomers (p. 101). Regardless of your situation, you will surely overcome because the end will reveal the glory of God. Jesus assures us, "These things I have spoken to you, that in Me you may have peace. In the world you will have tribulation, but be of good cheer, I have overcome the world" (John 16:33). The apostle Paul also reminds us that "in all these things we are more than conquerors through Him who loved us" (Romans 8:37).

If we persevere and trust God, the trials that God allows us to go through in life will unveil the glory that is in us. Jesus said, "But he who endures to the end shall be saved" (Matthew 24:13). Remember Hannah, who was childless and tormented by Peninnah, her husband's other wife, who had many children. Yet she endured and trusted God without doubt or concern. Not long after visiting the temple to present her request to the Lord, she was with child. God revealed His glory in her circumstance. She acknowledged the glory of God in her situation when she prayed.

> Then Hannah prayed and said: "My heart rejoices in the Lord; My horn is exalted in the Lord. I smile at my enemies, Because I rejoice in Your salvation. No one is holy like the Lord, For there is none besides You, Nor is there any rock like our God." (1 Samuel 2:1–2)

No challenges can prevent opportunities to reveal His glory from God's standpoint. In every situation, whether good or bad, ultimately the goal is the revelation of God's glory.

6

THE TIME OF GOD'S GLORY

The revelation of God's glory occurs at God's appointed time. His appointed time is a perfect time. God is timeless in the sense of being outside time altogether. In an article titled "What Is God's relationship to time?" (para. 10–12), Got Questions Ministries explains that God is spirit (John 4:24), and correspondingly, God is timeless rather than being eternal in time or being beyond time. Time was simply created by God as a limited part of His creation for accommodating the workings of His purpose in His disposable universe (2 Peter 3:10–12). Upon the completion of His creation activity, including the creation of time, what did God conclude? "God saw all that he had made, and it was very good" (Genesis 1:31). Indeed, God is spirit in the realm of timelessness rather than flesh in the sphere of time.

As believers, we have a deep sense of comfort knowing that God, though timeless and eternal, is in time with us right now; He is not unreachably transcendent but right here in this moment with us. And because He's in this moment, He can respond to our needs and prayers. Time does not control when God reveals His glory, nor could you hurry up nor slow down the time for God's readiness because He is Lord over time. God's glory has existed before time, still exists in time, and will exist after time because He is "the First and Last" (Isaiah 41:4; 44:6; 48:12), "the Beginning and End" (Revelation 21:6), "the one who is, was, and is to come" (Revelation 1:4; Revelation 1:8), and "King of the Ages" (1 Timothy 1:17; Revelation 15:3).

Time does not control when God reveals His glory, nor could you hurry up nor slow down the time for God's readiness because He is Lord over time.

God's time is the perfect timing for the revelation of

His glory. God gives us hopes and dreams for certain things to happen in our lives, but He doesn't always allow us to see the exact timing of His plan. Though very frustrating, not knowing the precise timing of the revelation of His glory influences what keeps us in the program.

> Now a certain man was sick, Lazarus of Bethany, the town of Mary and her sister Martha. It was that Mary who anointed the Lord with fragrant oil and wiped His feet with her hair, whose brother Lazarus was sick. Therefore the sisters sent to Him, saying, "Lord, behold, he whom You love is sick." When Jesus heard that, He said, "This sickness is not unto death, but for the glory of God, that the Son of God may be glorified through it." Now Jesus loved Martha and her sister and Lazarus. So, when He heard that he was sick, He stayed two more days in the Place where He was … Then Jesus said to them plainly, "Lazarus is dead. And I am glad for your sakes that I was not there,

that you may believe. Nevertheless let us go to him." (John 11:11–14)

In the preceding scriptures, Jesus got word that his friend Lazarus was critically ill. Much to His disciple's astonishment, Jesus didn't run to heal him. Instead, he deliberately waited for two more days. When Jesus arrived in Bethany, the home of Lazarus and his two sisters, Jesus learned that Lazarus had died four days earlier. Ultimately Jesus revealed the glory of God to Mary and Martha and the people standing by when He raised Lazarus from the dead by calling his name. Jesus was never early, never late, but always on time, the time of glory. Our timing isn't God's timing. God's perfect timing does two things. It grows our faith as we are forced to wait and trust in God and it makes certain that He, and He alone, gets the glory and praise for pulling us through. There are times when we might give up if we knew how long it was going to take, but when we accept God's timing, we can learn to live in hope and enjoy our lives while God is working on our problems. We know that God's plan for our lives is good, and when we entrust ourselves to Him, we can experience total peace and happiness.

At the right time, God will provide for your need. The critical thing to understand is that God knows your need and knows the perfect time to meet that need. It is time for you to laugh. Sarah was childless until she was ninety years old. God promised she was going to conceive a child. Considering that she has passed the age of childbearing, she laughed at the promise unknown to her that the time of glory has been set.

> Then they said to him, "Where is Sarah your wife?" So he said, "Here, in the tent." And He said, "I will certainly return to you according to the time of life, and behold, Sarah your wife shall have a son." (Sarah was listening in the tent door which was behind him.) Now Abraham and Sarah were old, well advanced in age; and Sarah had passed the age of childbearing. Therefore Sarah laughed within herself, saying, "After I have grown old, shall I have pleasure, my lord being old also?" And the Lord said to Abraham, "Why did Sarah laugh, saying, 'Shall I surely bear a child, since I am

old?' Is anything too hard for the Lord? At the appointed time I will return to you, according to the time of life, and Sarah shall have a son." (Genesis 18:9–14)

God revealed His glory at the appointment time and in an impossible situation of Sarah's and Abraham's physical inability to bear a child.

> For Sarah conceived and bore Abraham a son in his old age, at the set time of which God had spoken to him. And Abraham called the name of his son who was born to him—whom Sarah bore to him—Isaac ... Now Abraham was one hundred years old when his son Isaac was born to him. And Sarah said, "God has made me laugh, and all who hear will laugh with me." (Genesis 21:2–3, 5–6)

The time of glory is the appointment time when everything works together for you to the glory of God (Romans 8:28). It is the time that nothing or nobody can reverse. So it is worthwhile to wait and trust God for your time of glory.

Therefore the Lord will wait, that He may be gracious to you; And therefore He will be exalted, that He may have mercy on you. For the Lord is a God of justice; Blessed are all those who wait for Him. (Isaiah 30:18)

You need to serve or be a useful tool in the hands of God while you are waiting for the time of glory. Waiting, trusting, and serving is your sustenance to when God will reveal His glory in your life.

At the Time of Glory, God Will Provide

God has made everything beautiful in its time (Ecclesiastes 3:11). So at the time of glory, God must manifest His glory in your life. God is never late. He is always on time, and the scripture tells us, "And we know that all things work together for good to them that love God, to them who are the called according to His purpose" (Romans 8:28).

"In all things" is reassuring. It means that no matter the circumstance, there are only two qualifiers for God to work all things together for our good. First, He works for "the good of those who love Him." If you love God, you can trust that He is working for your good, and your welfare is paramount to Him. Second, He works for "those who are called according to His purpose." He has called you for a purpose, and His plans for you to fulfill that purpose are sure.

When my wife, Dayo, and I got married, like a young, ambitious couple who had their plans mapped out, we had planned to get pregnant a year after our marriage. A few years into our marriage, nothing happened. Despite what we perceived as a delay, we did not compromise our love and commitment to serve.

My wife's history of irregular menstrual cycles contributed to our delay. We consulted with a gynecologist, and she started treatment, but after several attempts to get pregnant, nothing happened because it was not the time of God's glory. Finally, after relocating to the United States, with better medical treatment, she was able to get pregnant. Unfortunately, the pregnancy was ectopic, thereby losing one of her fallopian tubes, which according to the doctor reduced her chances of getting pregnant by 50 percent. After this incident, my wife got pregnant several times, but they all resulted in miscarriages. However, we continued to trust God and waited on Him.

We were referred to a fertility specialist who, after several tests were carried out, explained the underlying problem. He explained that my wife produces immature eggs, so even when she ovulates and fertilizes them, it results in miscarriages. IVF was advised with treatment to produce matured eggs. My wife and I agreed, and we decided to try it, and of course, we trusted God for a successful result. A few weeks after the procedure, the pregnancy test returned positive with triplets. This good news was short-lived because my wife was immediately admitted to the hospital because of the bulging of her womb resulting from fluid. The doctors could not figure out what was going on. Immediately, my prayer changed from "Bless us with a child" to "God, save my wife." In the end, my wife miscarried again. We then decided to stop all medical interventions and continue to wait on God. Six months after the miscarriage, my wife got pregnant again, which was the beginning of our miracle. After ten years of marriage, we gave birth to a healthy baby boy. Today, we are proud parents of three boys—ages fifteen, thirteen, and ten—all to the glory of God.

God in our lives has made everything beautiful in

its time. God was right on time to manifest His glory through us and our marriage. There is always glory ahead when you love God and fulfill His purpose. In other words, in your Christian journey, there are a place, a situation, and a time of glory ahead.

AT THE TIME OF GLORY, GOD WILL DELIVER YOU

Deliverance is inevitable at the time of the revelation of the glory of God. Your expected deliverance will be conclusive at the time of glory.

> You will arise and have mercy on Zion; For the time to favor her, Yes, the set time, has come. For Your servants take pleasure in her stones, And show favor to her dust. So the [a]nations shall fear the name of the Lord, And all the kings of the earth Your Glory. For the Lord shall build up Zion; He shall appear in His Glory. (Psalm 102:13–16)

Regardless of how many times you have been a subject of ridicule because of what you are going through, God's time of glory will deliver and silence your antagonists.

> Do not rejoice over me, my enemy; When I fall, I will arise; When I sit in darkness, The Lord will be a light to me ... Then she who is my enemy will see, And shame will cover her who said to me, "Where is the Lord your God?" My eyes will see her; Now she will be trampled down Like mud in the streets. (Micah 7:8, 10)

He is God yesterday, today, and forevermore. Hence, the revelation of the glory of God in our life is always at the perfect time. He was never too late nor too early to reveal His glory in the past. He will not be too early or late in manifesting His glory today. And He will not be too early or too late in the future for His glory to manifest.

AT THE TIME OF GLORY, GOD WILL LIFT YOU UP

God has the power to lift you up without hindrance. To be lifted or exalted by God is to be given a new status by God, and it happens unexpectedly at God's appointed time. So for each lifting you got, it originated from God. He arranged it and guaranteed it happened (Psalm 75:6–7). Do you doubt it? Ask the individuals who have not been advanced for quite a while. God's support upon a man conveys His glory on him. Lifting, exaltation, or promotion most times comes after a period of paying the price of waiting.

> But those who wait on the Lord Shall renew their strength; They shall mount up with wings like eagles, They shall run and not be weary, They shall walk and not faint. (Isaiah 40:31)

The time of glory is when the God of heaven has decided to lift you up such that no scheme of the enemy shall prosper in your life. This is seen in the account of Jesus Christ by apostle Paul.

> Let this mind be in you which was also in Christ Jesus, who, being in the form of God, did not consider it robbery to be equal with God, but made Himself of no reputation, taking the form of a

bondservant, and coming in the likeness of men. And being found in appearance as a man, He humbled Himself and became obedient to the point of death, even the death of the cross. Therefore God also has highly exalted Him and given Him the name which is above every name, that at the name of Jesus every knee should bow, of those in heaven, and of those on earth, and of those under the earth, and that every tongue should confess that Jesus Christ is Lord, to the glory of God the Father. (Philippians 2:5–11)

Jesus's lifting demonstrated the peak of the revelation of God's glory at the perfect time when all hope seems lost. The scriptures revealed how Jesus endured to pay the price required for God's lifting. What did He do to experience lifting at the time of glory?

- **No reputation** – *King James Dictionary* defines *reputation* as a "good name, the credit, honor, or character derived from a favorable public opinion or esteem. Reputation is a valuable property or right that should never be violated." Therefore, to experience God's glory at the perfect time, you must purge yourself of whatever you have or procured before God. The reputations of those who will be lifted are in God's hands. He owns it as much as He owns everything in this world. Therefore, before God, you should remain no one.

- **Bondservant of Christ** – The word *bondservant* is the translation of the Greek word *doulos,* which means "one who is submissive to, and entirely at the disposal of, his master; a slave." Other translations use the word *servant* or *bondservant.* So the apostle Paul explains when he referred to Tychicus as a beloved brother, faithful minister, and fellow servant in the Lord (Colossians 4:7). Both words are used as Paul refers to Tychicus as a *diakonos*—one who serves as a church servant. Second, he is a fellow slave (bondservant) of Christ in His work with Paul. Being a bondservant of Christ is the position or mentality you have to expect if God is to keep lifting you.

- **Humility** – In research from YourDictionary Staff, humility is the quality of being humble and means putting another person's needs before your own and thinking of others before yourself. It also means not drawing attention to yourself and acknowledging that you are not always right (yourdictionary.com). Jesus Christ is an embodiment of humility, and He prioritized others' needs ahead of his well-being for God to lift him. Therefore, humble yourselves under the mighty hand of God so that He may exalt you in due time (1 Peter 5:6). Humility is the clothing you need to put on to provoke your lifting at God's perfect time.

- **Obedience** – Obedience means hearing the Word of God and acting on it. It implies aligning our will with God's will and doing what God has asked us to do. It is when you completely surrender to His authority and base your decisions and actions on His Word. That was what Jesus Christ did before God lifted him. Jesus Christ obeyed even unto the death of the cross, which was the most despicable death, and God raised Him. When you obey God, whether it makes sense or doesn't, you position yourself for divine lifting.

There is the notion that time is against you, but the truth is that nobody is too old to be lifted or elevated in their endeavors. God can shine His glory at night or early. So how long have you been waiting for your lifting or promotion? Do not lose hope. Glorious days are ahead of you, the hand of God will surely lift you at His appointed time, and no one will stop you from reaching the top. Therefore, it is expedient that you have a good relationship with God, who can lift you.

7

THERE IS GLORY AHEAD

The glory ahead is the latter glory, the glory of greatness that comes in the latter days of your life when everyone has already concluded on you or written you off in destiny. In all things, give thanks to God. Why am I giving thanks to God, especially when I am in the wrong place, in a hopeless situation, or when the time is against me? The simple answer is that there is glory ahead. Paul understands that there is glory ahead when he encourages the churches at Galatia. He urged them not to get tired of doing what is good because there is reaping at the right time (Galatians 6:9). Glory ahead connotes that your present situation is not your final destination. The glory of God is the solution for every reproach anyone will ever face on earth. There is always a manifestation of God's glory awaiting your sufferings, so never give up until you have seen the glory. No matter the challenge you might be going through, there are good times ahead, which shall be far greater than the challenge you are going through now. There is glory ahead! God has kept glory for your life, your family, your future, and His church—not

> *No matter the challenge you might be going through, there are good times ahead, which shall be far greater than the challenge you are going through now.*

struggles, accidents, bondage, or disease. Paul wrote to hint at the glory that God has kept ahead for us. "Eye has not seen, nor ear heard, Nor have entered into the heart of man The things which God has prepared for those who love Him" (1 Corinthians 2:9).

Paul's statements made it very clear to the believers in Corinth that the glory ahead is beyond human comprehension and is there for many generations of believers. Hence, "the sufferings of this present time are not worthy to be compared with the glory which shall be revealed in us. For the earnest expectation of the creation eagerly waits for the revealing of the sons of God" (Romans 8:19). Glory ahead implies the following assurances.

Your Story Will Change to Glory

Glory ahead is an assurance that your story must change. Your story in the present is not permanent because the glory ahead will reverse it. Your story now may be that you are waiting to get pregnant, you are unemployed or waiting to get married, or you are depressed or limited in life. The good news is that there is glory ahead that must change your story to glory. The Bible tells us about Hannah, whose story changed from barrenness to fruitfulness. Hannah was one of two wives of Elkanah, and she was childless while Elkanah's other wife, Peninnah, had sons and daughters. She continuously provoked Hannah to make her miserable because the Lord had closed her womb (1 Samuel 1:6–7). One day, when Hannah could no longer bear the pain of her empty womb, she went to the temple to present her supplication to the Lord. She cried out to the Lord and wept bitterly. She was so distraught that she made a promise to the Lord in her request for a son.

Then she made a vow and said, "O Lord of hosts, if You will indeed look on the affliction of Your maidservant and remember me, and not forget Your maidservant, but will give Your maidservant a male child, then I will give him to the Lord all the days of his life, and no razor shall come upon his head." (1 Samuel 1:11)

Not long after she visited the temple to present her request to the Lord, she was with a child. Then she continued describing the glorious God.

"The Lord kills and makes alive; He brings down to the grave and brings up. The Lord makes poor and makes rich; He brings low and lifts up. He raises the poor from the dust And lifts the beggar from the ash heap, To set them among princes And make them inherit the throne of glory. "For the pillars of the earth are the Lord's, And He has set the world upon them. He will guard the feet of His saints, But the wicked shall be silent in darkness.

"For by strength no man shall prevail."'"
(1 Samuel 2:6-9)

Hannah's story changed to glory. Her old song of torment changed to a new song to give glory to God. What is your situation now? Your current condition cannot outweigh your future glory. Your afflictions, sufferings, and disappointments are not permanent. "For our light affliction, which is but for a moment, is working for us a far more exceeding and eternal weight of glory" (2 Corinthians 4:17).

This scripture assures you that challenging times can never be permanent in your life and God will bring you out of hard times because your current trial is just a setup for the latter glory. Always remember that your condition in the present is not permanent because there is glory ahead that will bring about an unprecedented turnaround of your situation to the glory of God.

THE BEST IS YET TO COME

Glory ahead implies the best is yet to come for you in all your endeavors. The blessing of God is progressive. That is, looking ahead to glory, your yesterday should not be better than your tomorrow. It does not matter how you look today, who you are, or what you have. The glory ahead will bring better days. Isaac's life exemplifies this implication. There was a famine in the land, and God warned Isaac not to go to Egypt but to settle in Gerar as an alien; God will be with him and bless him and his descendants here, fulfilling his oath to Abraham. "Then Isaac sowed in that land, and reaped in the same year a hundredfold; and the Lord blessed him. The man began to prosper, and continued prospering until he became very prosperous" (Genesis 26:12–13).

While other people were leaving the land to avoid famine, God warned Isaac against relocation because there was glory ahead for Isaac. The Bible stated that Isaac was blessed, and his blessing was progressive that the Philistines became envious of him (Genesis 26:14). Tomorrow will be better, so look forward to tomorrow with the assurance of greater glory. "'The glory of this latter house shall be greater than of the former,' saith the LORD of hosts. 'And in this place will I give peace,' saith the LORD of hosts'" (Haggai 2:9).

What is ahead of you is much better and very significant, so don't settle for where you are now. Elisha was a wealthy farmer, but a mantle would fall upon him, and he eventually arose as a double-portioned anointed prophet. You may not be able to see anything good now, but God has kept the best for you. All things are glorious now, but your situation will change from one level of glory to another. Glory ahead typifies that God has destined you to go from glory to glory. "But we all, with unveiled face, beholding as in a mirror the glory of the Lord, are being transformed into the same image from glory to glory, just as by the Spirit of the Lord" (1 Corinthians 3:18). Your past may not have been so good, but the glory ahead will bring you joy unspeakable that will dwarf your past. God has saved the best for you. The latter glory awaits you.

THE GLORY AHEAD MEANS YOU WILL END WELL AND FINISH STRONG

There was a glory of David that could not finish the temple, but the latter glory of Solomon built the temple and finished it. "So Solomon built the temple and finished it" (1 Kings 6:14). There is always glory ahead, and whether the place is conducive or not, it will manifest; whether the situation is palatable or not, it will manifest; whether the time is favorable or not, it will manifest.

REFERENCE LIST

Ballenger, M. (May 14, 2016). *What Is the Glory of God according to the Bible?* ApplyGodsWord. Com, retrieved December 27, 2022, from https://applygodsword.com/what-is-the-glory-of-god-according-to-the-bible/.

"Examples of Humility Expressed in Different Ways" (n.d.). Examples.yourdictionary.com, retrieved December 27, 2022, https://examples.yourdictionary.com/examples-of-humility.html.

Gill, J. (2022). *Exposition of the Bible.* Publisher.

GotQuestions.org. (June 7, 2010). "What Is God's Relationship to Time?" retrieved December 27, 2022, from https://www.gotquestions.org/God-time.html.

Grant, N. (2017). John 11:40 Bible exposition commentary, retrieved April 23, 2022, from https://versebyversecommentary.com/2017/11/07/john-1140/.

Ligonier Ministries. "Christ the Glory of God" (December 18, 2017), retrieved May 20, 2022, from https://www.ligonier.org/learn/devotionals/christ-glory-god.

Munroe, M. (2001). *The Purpose and Power of God's Glory*. Destiny Image Pub.

Piper, J. (August 30, 1980). "How to Do Good So That God Gets the Glory," retrieved December 23, 2022, from https://www.desiringgod.org/messages/how-to-do-good-so-that-god-gets-the-glory.

Piper, J. (November 30, 2017). "The Meaning of the Manger," retrieved December 19, 2022, from https://www.desiringgod.org/articles/the-meaning-of-the-manger.

Piper, J. (September 1, 2021). "We Become Like the Videos We Behold," retrieved October 23, 2022, from https://

www.desiringgod.org/interviews/we-become-like-the-videos-we-behold.

Rosenberg, Matt. (July 13, 2019). "The 5 Themes of Geography," retrieved June 23, 2022, from https://www.thoughtco.com/five-themes-of-geography-1435624.

Tripp, P. (August 20, 2018). "The Doctrine of Glory," retrieved November 23, 2022, from https://www.paultripp.com/articles/posts/the-doctrine-of-glory-article?gclid=Cj0KCQiA64GRBhCZARIsA HOLriLXjVFmi65glTzBL3Hi1kvBzBfWMoTLtcE YMEQZVgqpW6APJY_9cBwaAkFiEALw_wcB.

Printed in the United States
by Baker & Taylor Publisher Services